You Could Be Making $100 an Hour Doing Home Inspections

Brian Price

Contents

Introduction

From a young age, people tell us that if something sounds too good to be true, it usually is. The title of this book, *You Could Be Making $100 an Hour Doing Home Inspections*, sounds like a statement that could easily fit into that realm. After all, that is a lot of money. How many times in your life have you been paid $100 an hour? To think that you could be trained and getting paid for doing professional home inspections in just a few months may add even more to the skepticism. I'm here to tell you that it's not too good to be true. All of this is possible. Home inspections are being done right now in your community, in your town, and you could be a part of it. If you are looking for a new career or just need a second income to make it in today's world, becoming a home inspector could be just what you are looking for.

This book's title states that you could be making $100 an hour. I want to take some time now and explain to you how I came up with this figure. If you've ever had to pay for a home inspection you know they are not cheap. Average home inspections cost around $300-$400. By average I'm referring to a 3 bedroom, 2 bath single family home with up to 2000 square feet in living space. The average home inspection should take about 3 hours. Drive time to the worksite and compiling the report take some added time as well. If you charge $400 for the inspection and add to the equation a 30 minute drive time and another 30 minutes to write up the report, you got paid $400 for 4 hours work. That comes out to $100 an hour.

At times you should be able to make over $100 an hour. Let's say you inspect a brand new 4000 square foot house and the client wants a radon test done, which you can do for $90. The house has a lot of square footage and 4 bathrooms so you charge $590 for everything. The inspection is an easy one and the whole thing takes 4 hrs. You just made about $145 an hour. Unfortunately, there will be times you will make less than $100 an hour. You might run into a house that is not "average". Older houses especially can take more time. That same house you did for $400 wouldn't pay as much hourly if it took you 5 hrs to finish. At that rate you would make about $80 an hour, which is still an excellent wage.

It's conceivable that you could do two or more inspections in the same day. Some home inspectors do this and they might take home $800 or more in a single day. This won't happen every day, but it's something to keep in mind. Now that I have your attention with the pay home inspectors receive, I need to point out some other good reasons to become a home inspector.

Control: As a home inspector you will be your own boss. This means that you won't be answering to anyone but yourself. You create your own company policies and decide when you want to work and when you don't. If you need some time off for a vacation, schedule it in. Some people choose to keep their regular job and do inspections part-time. It's up to you. You can decide to do 2 inspections in a day or 2 inspections in a month.

Ease of entry: A great reason to become a home inspector is that you don't need to take expensive classes or college courses to become one. You can learn everything you need to know on your own. Plus you don't need a lot of money to get started. Not if you incorporate the use of my methods.

Finally, you don't need lots of time. Depending on how motivated you are I believe one could be trained and ready to start inspecting houses in as little as a few months.

There are a lot of home inspection training companies out there. They want you to believe that you need to take one of their courses, and pay the big costs associated with it. Some of these companies are charging thousands of dollars for their training courses. This is really the reason why I decided to write this book. I wanted everyone to know that there are alternative ways to learn how to inspect houses. It doesn't make sense to spend a lot of money on training and starting your business, just to find out later you don't really want to be a home inspector.

One reason you might have for not wanting to be a home inspector is if you are in poor health or not very limber. In this profession you will be called upon to climb up on ladders, crawl around in crawl spaces and look under sinks. If you think you would have trouble performing these tasks, home inspection may not be your thing. I do however see one solution to this problem. If you're married or have a significant other, you could get them to come along on the inspections with you. Maybe you could find a business partner and do 2 person inspections. You could finish twice as fast. If they are better at climbing and crawling around, let them perform those tasks.

Another thing that might make you not want to be a home inspector is if you're shy or not comfortable talking to people. You will be talking on the phone and talking in person. Sometimes there might be two or more people asking you questions as you do the inspection. If you don't like working with people, do yourself a favor and find another line of work. To be honest though, it's not that difficult. Many of your inspections will be done on your own with nobody else present.

My Qualifications

At this point I want to tell you a few things about myself and why I'm qualified to write this book. In 2006 I successfully started a business in Minnesota called Independent Home Inspection. That same year I became a licensed home inspector for the state of Wisconsin.

Although I am a very good home inspector, I am not an expert on home inspection. I haven't performed thousands of inspections yet and I don't have the knowledge of someone with 25 years of home inspecting experience. That's ok. That's not what this book is about. If you want a book about doing expert inspections, there are dozens of them out there. In fact, you should probably read a few of them. This book is different. This book is about taking a complete beginner and having them trained and inspecting houses in as little time as possible and as inexpensively as possible. In fact this book is one of a kind. No other book that I know of describes the methods I am suggesting when it comes to getting your education.

I've been down the road of learning how to be a home inspector. It isn't easy. Nobody wants to let you in on their secret. Who can really blame them? Do you really think they want you competing for their $100 an hour? I'm going to tell you the ins and outs and then let you decide. Before dropping $1400 or more on a training course, I think everyone should at least read this book. I've been talking about home inspections so much that it's probably about time I explain what one is

What is a Home Inspection?

A home inspection is a visual examination of the readily accessible systems and components of a house. A home inspection is done in accordance to a certain set of standards using normal operator controls such as the thermostat, toilet flush handle, and hot/cold water handles. Most home inspectors use the standards set forth by the American Society of Home Inspectors or ASHI. Readily accessible means inspectors don't look inside walls, behind furniture or under carpets. Typically a home inspection should take around 3 hours. The end result of every home inspection is the report. Usually delivered to the client electronically, the report explains what was uncovered during the inspection, both good and bad. The realtor and buyer then use this information to decide if they want to go ahead and make the purchase. Later in this book I explain the whole process of a home inspection more thoroughly.

When Do You Need One?

More and more often, states and communities are requiring that anyone who puts their house up for sale on the open real estate market has it professionally inspected first. This basically assures that the quality of housing in a community remains high and buyers don't get stuck with a house that has major issues. Of course it also depends on how good the home inspector is. If an inspector doesn't know what to look for, it won't matter how many times it's inspected. It wouldn't be uncommon for the same house to be inspected 2 or even 3 different times, by 2 or 3 different home inspectors throughout its sales process. This is because there are many different kinds of home inspections. The more different ones you know, the more you'll be able to do. The more you do the more money you'll make.

Most people I come in contact with in this business confuse a home inspection with a city "code" inspection. They are not even remotely comparable. Only people who work for the city or county can perform a code inspection. Code inspections are not typically done when transferring the sale of a home to another home buyer. A home inspection isn't focused on rules and regulations; it's more about the overall property condition.

Another common thing that people confuse with a home inspection is a home appraisal. Once again, these are two completely different things. An appraisal deals more with determining a property's value. Home inspectors don't determine a home's square footage. Again, they deal more with the homes overall condition.

How Much Do They Cost?

The cost of a home inspection depends on a few factors. Size is the main factor. Most home inspectors in all areas of the United States will charge about $300 for a house up to 2000 square feet in size. Call around in your area and see what the average base price is. As the square footage increases, so does the price. Adding $100 for each additional 1000 square feet is acceptable.

Age is another factor. Older houses are harder to inspect and take more time. You will want to charge an extra $50 or $75 for a house 30 years old or more. Distance to the inspection should be considered when determining the inspection fee. You wouldn't want to drive 40 miles each way and not figure in your gas costs, especially with today's high gas prices.

As a home inspector you can perform other tests on houses that will generate more income for you. Some services you might consider adding could be; radon testing, lead paint testing, water testing, and mold testing. Be sure that you are trained and qualified before you attempt these services.

The Different Types of Inspections

First there's the <u>pre-purchase inspection,</u> also known as a buyers' inspection. This is where a prospective buyer hires an independent home inspector to evaluate the potential purchase. This is a very thorough inspection and should last 3 hours or more. All of the major components of the house are looked at as well as hundreds of other items.

Then there's the <u>pre-listing</u> inspection. This is an evaluation sellers have done prior to putting their home up for sale. The purpose is to determine whether there are any faults or conditions in the home that can be corrected before a "truth in housing" or "buyers" inspection. The homeowner really just wants to know the homes condition before any surprises are uncovered.

Then there is the <u>truth in sale of housing</u> inspection. More and more communities are now requiring by law that the home seller have one done prior to selling. The requirements are different from one city to the next but they all look at major safety and code issues. These inspections are not meant to be comprehensive, all inclusive inspections, like a buyers' inspection. They generally take half as long and look at fewer items so they usually cost about half as much. If you plan on doing these types of inspections, you're going to need a license. You can get a license by passing a home inspection test issued by that city or community.

There are a few other types of inspections that you could do. HUD and the VA may have needs for inspectors in your area. If you want to work for FEMA you could become a disaster housing inspector and follow natural disasters likes hurricanes and floods. After hurricane Katrina, New Orleans needed several thousand homes inspected. Search around on different government websites and see which ones are looking for home inspectors.

Finding work in down markets

One concern you might have is: How do home inspectors find work in a bad housing market? A good solution to this would be to focus on doing inspections for home investors. Even in down markets, there are always people buying up properties for investment. People buy when the market is flooded and houses are cheap. Investors often look to home inspectors to help them understand exactly what it is they are buying. You just have to change with the market. You just need to follow the work. Keep in mind that you will have to look a little harder for inspection work during these times. This means working harder than the other inspectors.

Another area you could change your focus to is one year warranty inspections. When someone buys a brand new home from a builder, they typically get a one year warranty on the home. This covers any issues the house may have incurred over the year. New houses settle into the ground and lots of issues can present themselves. Find out where the houses that were built last year are. Stick a flyer on their front door about 2 months before the warranty expires.

A Typical Home Inspection Walkthrough

Now that you know the different types of home inspections, I thought it would be helpful if I walked you through a typical buyer's inspection. I will explain all the basics from the initial call requesting the inspection to collecting your fee and delivering the report. Each inspection you do will be different from the last one. You will quickly build on your experience and get better at inspecting each time. The First one or two inspections will be nerve racking to say the least. By the time you get a few jobs under your belt you should start feeling more comfortable. The order in which you choose to inspect the different components of a house is completely up to you. I have based the following inspection walkthrough on what I have found works best.

The Phone Call

Almost every home inspection you do will be prompted by a phone call. It's best to use a good quality landline phone with an answering machine; however a cell phone will work. Since you will be operating out of your home, apartment, or on the go with a cell phone it's important that you are always ready for your calls. This means you're going to want it quiet. The last thing you want is a barking Chihuahua or a loud television show on in the background of your call.

Answer your calls politely using your business name. For example, I would say" Independent Home Inspection, how can I help you?" Practice trying to sound professional and enthusiastic. If you sound rude or uninterested that caller will probably just hang up and call the next inspector on their list. Avoid letting your answering machine answer your calls. It's my experience that people leave messages but usually set an inspection up with the first live person they can get on the phone. That's usually the next caller on their list, not you.

There are several things you're going to need to ask the caller in order to book the inspection. Therefore you need to have an order sheet and pen or pencil next to the phone that you will fill in when someone calls you. An order sheet is just a list of things you need to know. Things like; client's name, address of the property being inspected, square footage, age of house, who will be present at the inspection, and phone numbers. You will have to use the information you gather to set a price. Make sure you discuss the price before you end the call.

Send out a contract for them to look over and have them sign it and have it waiting. You can find examples of contracts for home inspectors online or at office supply stores. If you don't like the idea of sending out a contract in the mail, you can bring one along and have them sign it when you arrive on site. Mailing one beforehand just saves you time and lets the client go over the contract on their own time. Whichever way you do it, just make sure you get a signed contract before you begin the inspection.

It's a really good idea to ask the client or realtor if all the utilities are on so you can do a complete inspection. If the utilities are shut off you won't be able to inspect all the components. For example if the water is shut off you won't be able to do a proper inspection on the plumbing. The inspection report would read "water shut off, couldn't inspect plumbing"

Imagine how upset the client would be. Especially when you have to go back and re-inspect the plumbing later (and charge them another $100). Avoid the hassle. Make sure the utilities are on. In some instances it won't always be possible to have the utilities on. This is usually the case when the home has been foreclosed on or the occupants have moved out.

It's very important that the client has all the areas you need to inspect clear from any boxes or belongings. This mostly relates to the furnace area, crawlspace entrances, and attic access areas. If you can't get to an area, you can't inspect it. If you have to be called back to finish inspecting an area that was unreachable, you will want to charge at least $100 to come back out and finish up. Now set a date and time that works for both of you and get ready for your upcoming inspection.

Before Leaving For the Inspection

On the day of the inspection, you need to make sure you are well prepared. Clear your mind of any stress and focus on the upcoming inspection. Nothing else in the world should matter now for the next 3 hours or so. You owe it to your client to do the best job you possibly can do for them.

Appearances do make a difference. Your vehicle should be clean and free of dents. At first you probably won't have company uniforms. Just wear something nice and clean. Try to at least look the part. Maybe wear a tool belt and work boots, with jeans. Now gather up all the tools and items that you will need for the inspection and put them in your vehicle. Items you'll want to remember include; a contract for the client to sign (if they haven't signed it yet), Inspection reports, a clipboard, 2 pens, business cards, a receipt book (available at office supply stores), and your tools. Another item that is strongly suggested is breath mints. One thing I would never do is chew gum or smoke during the inspection, as this appears unprofessional. If you have to smoke, I would do it well before your arrival. The smell of cigarettes lingers a long time and some people are turned off, even offended by it.

Each inspection you do should be considered an audition of sorts. Your goal is to do a good job and impress the client so they will call on you for their next inspection. Or better yet, refer you to their friends and family as well.

What to Do Upon Arrival

Make sure you arrive at the property on time. The last thing you want is to have anyone waiting for you. That wouldn't help you get a referral. Greet your client and anyone else there appropriately. Hand out your business card to everyone there. If you happen to get there early, walk around the property and start doing some of your exterior observations until the client arrives. This is the moment that the inspection actually begins.

Start the inspection by walking around the perimeter of the house two separate times. On your first pass around take a close look at the sloping of the ground and how it relates to the foundation of the house. The slope of the ground should be away from the foundation so that when it rains, water is directed away from the house. Take a look at all the gutters and downspouts. Are they connected at all their joints? Are the gutters plugged up with leaves and debris? Are the downspouts directing the rainwater away from the house at least 6 feet? It's amazing how many leaky basements could be remedied by fixing these little things. Many homeowners go years wondering why their basement leaks, while tiny trees grow all along their gutters.

Check for what type of electrical service the house has. It either has overhead wires or an underground cable. If the house has overhead wires coming in, check to see that they are the proper height. Make sure there are no trees growing into the wires. Are the wires brought into the house correctly? Don't worry at this point if you don't know anything about what to look for when inspecting. All you're really doing is following a report and checking off the boxes. If you understand the report it's hard to miss anything. I'll explain more about that later on.

Continue on your first pass and check the condition of the doors, windows, siding, decks, sidewalks, stairs, and handrails. Probe wood areas where you suspect water damage with an awl or sharp instrument. This could be where wood stairs meet the ground, or around wooden window sills where water can collect. Turn on any outside water faucets (hose bibs). Make sure the water flows out. If you have a water pressure gage you can check the house water pressure here. Sometimes these hose bibs are shut off. This is done in colder climates to prevent the pipes from freezing and cracking during the winter months. If you find this to be the case, go inside and find the shut off valve. As long as it's not cold out, turn on the faucet and re check.

If the house you are inspecting has air conditioning, you will find the a/c condenser unit outside, usually on the side or back of the house. It's pretty easy to spot. It is a large metal boxlike structure with a big fan that blows air straight up. Is the unit on a sturdy slab? Is it on a level surface? Is there an emergency shut off switch located nearby? Is the unit being choked off by tall grass or bushes? All of these things affect its performance. Never operate the air conditioning if the outside temperature is 65 degrees or less. The unit could be damaged.

Now it's time to make your second pass around the house. This time concentrate on the roof and the conditioning of its covering. What kind of material is the roof covering made of? Is it asphalt shingles? Is it wood shakes? Look closely at the surface for defects or areas that could be prone to leaking. Roofs tend to leak around areas that have penetrations through them. Areas like the chimney, or where plumbing vents go through. Make sure the chimney is the proper height above the roofline. If there is a brick and mortar chimney, check it for areas that show deterioration. Many home inspectors like to walk up on the roof and get a close up look. If you feel comfortable doing this you should think about doing it as well. Be very careful up on roofs and stay off them when they are wet. You could easily slip and fall off. Another reason to stay off roofs is that they are sometimes rotted underneath and you could fall right through. In order to get a better look, I recommend using a pair of binoculars. Most leaks in the roof can be detected from the underside. When you are up in the attic, look for water stains on the underside of the roof sheathing. Water stains could be active or from an old leak that has been repaired. Make sure you can tell the difference and make sure you call it out in your report. When all of your outside work is done it's time to head inside. If there is a basement, I usually head down there

The Basement

The basement is where you will find many of the major systems of the house. This would include the furnace, hot water heater, electrical panel, and the plumbing. If the house you're inspecting doesn't have a basement, you'll find those components in other rooms throughout the house. You might find the furnace in the garage, or the electrical panel in a closet. Many times I've had to search pretty hard to find the different components.

Let's start by locating the furnace or the main heat source for the home. Is it a gas fired furnace or electric? Is it a boiler unit? If you have no idea what I'm talking about, don't worry. Just remember that you will be able to tell the difference soon. I will show you how to train and learn the job in a later chapter.

Now locate the hot water heater. Is it gas fired or electric? Does it have all its safety features? Is it located in a room where someone sleeps and could get carbon monoxide poisoning? Many newer homes use on-demand hot water heaters. Is that the case with the house you're looking at? Hot water heaters need a close look, they usually last only 6-8 years.

Next you will locate the electrical panel. Always be extremely careful when working around electricity and service panels. The electrical systems of a home are the most dangerous thing you will encounter. If you aren't careful you could be seriously injured or even killed. Home inspectors are required to unscrew the electrical panel cover and take it off. This needs to be done so you can look inside and make sure everything is wired properly. Many panels are wired wrong and if this is the case, write it up on the report. You would write in your report that they need to bring in an electrician for further investigation.

Other areas in the basement to inspect include; the plumbing, floor joists, main house beam, support columns, house drain, foundation walls, stairs, and the clothes washer and dryer. Plastic dryer venting is a fire hazard in all communities. At high temperatures it melts and starts on fire. Venting should be made of metal and approved by the local plumbing authority. Also, dryers should never be vented directly into the basement. They should be vented to the outside of the house. Venting indoors creates excess moisture and could lead to rotting or mold. Remember, everything that needs inspecting is on your inspection report checklist so you really can't miss anything. After finishing up the basement, it's time to head back upstairs.

The Upstairs

Start with the kitchen. Head right over to the sink. Turn on the hot water and make sure it gets hot. Turn on the cold water. Look around the faucet area and make sure it isn't leaking anywhere. Fill the sink with water and then let it drain. While it's draining, look underneath the sink and check for leaking drain pipes. Look on the counter top for all the electrical outlets. Are there enough outlets to service the kitchen? Are all the outlets within 3 feet of the sink G.F.C.I. type outlets? If the house has an exhaust fan over the stove, turn it on. Does it work? Does it exhaust to the outdoors? If it doesn't, write it up. Do a basic check of all the appliances, especially the dishwasher. If there is a dishwasher you will have to fill it with water and run it through the drain cycle.

The next area I would go to would be the attic. Climb up on your ladder and pop off the attic access cover. If you're not comfortable climbing up into the attic, just peek inside with a powerful flashlight. I like to crawl around in the attic and get a good look. Check the insulation. Is it adequate? What type is it? Check for areas that leak by looking closely for any water stains or wood rot. If you do go into the attic, watch where you are going. If you happen to miss a joist, you could end up falling through the ceiling. Remember, you are responsible for any damage you cause to the house. Hopefully you carry insurance. Be aware of any dangerous electrical wiring. Many homeowners try to do their own electrical work. Sometimes you will find improper or exposed wiring in the attic. Be safe. Keep in mind that a lot of the things you will write up in your report will be improper repairs and construction work done by the homeowner. This is especially true when it comes to minor plumbing and electrical projects. Many times homeowners don't want to hire a professional and they do the work themselves. If work was done on a house and done properly, you should be able to see if there was ever a permit issued to do the work. In fact, it's a good idea to check with the local building authority to see if there were ever permits issued to the property you are inspecting.

The final areas you will look at are the bedrooms, bathrooms, hallways, stairs, closets, and all the other rooms in the house. You will be looking at things like; electrical outlet placement, straightness of the walls and floors, window condition, doors, and floor coverings. Just like you did in the kitchen, run the water in the bathrooms and check the plumbing for leaks. Don't forget the bathtub and shower. Bathrooms must have some type of ventilation. It could be a window or exhaust fan. The moisture created by showering needs to escape the house. If you don't see a fan or window, write it up.

When everything in the report has been addressed it's time to wrap it up and find the client so you can discuss your findings. This is just a verbal overview of your report. The actual report will be available for the client when you send it to them, usually by way of e-mail.

Delivery of the report

Depending on what type of report you use, your inspection may not be completed just yet. If you're using the old hand written style reports, simply finish it up on site and hand them their copy. This hand written styled report is fine but it's now the age of technology and computer generated reports are much better. Today's reports are sent electronically to the clients e mail address. Today's reports are colorful and contain digital photos for easier explanation of problem areas. In addition to the e mailed report, I would send them a copy on disc of the report in the mail. A few days later follow that up with a thank you postcard.

When you do your first couple of inspections, you're going to be nervous. Try to appear calm and confident. Slow down and act like you know what you're doing. The client is putting their trust in you. Besides, you should know what you're doing by now. Home inspectors don't need to be experts on everything, just knowledgeable about everything.

Remember, there are a lot more things to address in your report than I have spoken about here. Reading my inspection walkthrough doesn't make you a home inspector. It's just a basic overview of a typical home inspection. Its purpose is to give you a feel for how a real inspection is conducted.

My Personal Learning Experience

As I searched around learning about home inspection, I realized there were many different paths I could choose. One option I looked at was buying into a franchise. A franchise is really just a large corporation that lends out its name to you for a large buy-in fee and a percentage of your sales. It might be similar to buying a McDonald's restaurant. The franchisee would train me and supply all the reports, marketing, and advertising. Good idea if you have thousands of dollars and don't mind being at their mercy. I wanted more creative control. I wanted something that was unique to me. It also didn't help that I was low on cash.

Another option I found was attending a two week training course. Luckily I lived in a large urban area and there was a place I could attend nearby. If you live in a smaller town you might not be so lucky. It seemed like a pretty good way to get trained. That is until I saw that this option would cost me over $2700. Also, unless you're unemployed, it would be pretty hard to get two weeks off in a row from your current job if you have one.

Through further investigation I discovered that I could get the same content from those classes mailed to me in what is called a correspondence course. This option was less expensive but still a lot of money. They wanted $1400 for the at home course. This is the choice I decided to go with. If you do a search online for "home inspector training" the first pages that pop up are all training institutes selling their courses. It just seemed natural to go with one.

About a week later the course arrived on my doorstep, as promised. I opened the box and pulled everything out to look at it. I have to say I was a little disappointed. It seemed like a lot of money to pay for eight bulky vinyl 3-ring binders filled with photo copied material and some DVD's. The course was basically formatted into eight sections. They included; getting started, plumbing, electrical, structure and foundation, roofs, heating and air conditioning, insulation, and code compliance. There was even an outdated grainy VHS tape of a home inspection that looked like it was made some time back in the 1980's. I had to dig out an old VCR from my basement just to watch it. This, you should know, was from the "top" inspection school out there. What I'm basically trying to say is that there wasn't a lot of bang for the buck. Not $1400 worth.

This is how the course worked. You would read one of the eight sections at a time. Each section had some worksheets to fill in and a test at the end. The test was done online. It was basically open book and anyone could pass. After completing all eight sections, there was a final exam to take online. I passed it. A few weeks later I received in the mail a cheap looking certificate and a letter congratulating me. So now I have a certificate saying I'm trained. It's really just a useless piece of paper. You give them $1400; they give you a certificate saying that you're now trained. Not a bad deal, for them.

There's another way to get trained. A way of getting trained that none of the inspection schools want you to know anything about. A way where you can learn everything they teach and more. But most importantly, a way that won't cost you $1400. A way that's basically free. Let me explain.

The course I bought kept telling me that I should further read up on the subject they were teaching. This meant looking at materials outside the course. So when I was learning about roofs, I went to the library and checked out a few books on roofing. These library books combined contained much more information than just the course section on roofs by itself. When you read different books on the same subject by different authors, you get several viewpoints and interpretations on one subject. This in turn makes you better in that particular area.

Then I started looking up home inspection on YouTube. I found video after video of people showing how to inspect all the different components of a house. The video clips were up to date and again, several differing viewpoints on the same subject. Another great learning tool I discovered was television shows about houses. There are many different shows either on TV or accessible by the internet on demand. Home inspection is so popular that there are entire television series devoted to it. Libraries have many, many books just on home inspection and on starting a home inspection business. Libraries also have books you can check out on single subjects. Books on foundations, plumbing, siding, roofing, windows, insulation, electricity, deck and fence building, dry wall, painting a house, etc. Libraries also have copies of the National Electric Code, the Uniform Plumbing Code and books on local building codes. I was finding out so much about home inspecting through these avenues that I thought to myself: why didn't I save the $1400? I could've just read books and watched videos on the internet in the first place

As for practice exams, I found those as well. If you go to the website of the National Association of Certified Home Inspectors (NACHI) you will find a good practice exam. Other websites also have good practice exams. Search around on the internet and find different ones to take.

The key to becoming a home inspector does not lie in passing expensive courses. It lies in passing exams. The certificate you get for passing an inspection course does not ensure that you will pass the exams. This again raises the question "why spend $1400 on a correspondence course?"

Choose a Report

When it comes down to learning to be a home inspector, the first thing you need to do is pick a report style and learn that report inside out. As long as you can properly fill out and understand a report, you should be able to deliver your client a quality inspection. Go online and search for "home inspection reports". There are many companies out there selling many different styles of reports. The report website I liked a lot and used was reporthost.com. This particular website contains hundreds of real sample reports and it's easy to sign up. When I signed up, I got 15 free reports. Download some reports and start studying them. Most sites also contain hundreds of sample reports that you can view.

Another great place to download reports is from your local housing authority. In my case I went to the Saint Paul Minnesota truth in housing website. I found the section that was for housing evaluators and downloaded some reports. The best thing about finding a local city report is that the reports will be tailored to the codes and conditions where you will probably be inspecting. It doesn't make much sense to learn about earthquake safety issues when you're living in Wisconsin.

Now that you have a report, read it inside and out. Get comfortable with it.

Take each section one at a time and research everything the report is asking you. For instance, go to the section on electrical. Every report will have one. One of the items it will ask is whether the electrical service coming into the house is 120 volt or 220 volt. The answer to this question can be found with a little research on your part. I will save you the trouble of looking it up and just tell you that the answer is found by counting the number of overhead wires that are coming into the house. If you see two wires, the house has 120 volt. If you count 3 wires, the house has 220 volt. Almost every house you find will be 220 volt. If you see 120 volt, write it up. It's outdated by today's standards.

Look on your report at the section for the roof. It asks what type it is. Does it have a metal roof, wood shingles, asphalt shingles or clay tiles? After doing some research you'll be able to easily tell the difference. Then the report will ask about the condition of the roof. Let's say the house you're inspecting has asphalt shingles. The report will ask if you see any shingles or tiles missing. That's pretty easy to look for. Are the shingles starting to curl? Is there hail damage? You can learn the answer to all the questions being asked in the report by doing your research. Do this for each item in the report until you can comfortably understand each one.

Research the sections and questions on the report by looking on the internet and reading books on that subject. The report will ask: does the hot water heater have a temperature relief valve? Google temperature relief valve on the internet and you will instantly know what one is and where you will find one. If you can't find good articles online, read your library books.

Practice on Homes of Friends and Family

Now you should be ready to start doing practice home inspections. If you're a homeowner or renter, start by doing an inspection on the place where you live. If you have friends or family members that own houses, ask to inspect them. Take all your tools along as if you were doing a real inspection. Invite your host to go along on the inspection and encourage them to ask questions. If you don't know any of the answers go back and research them back at your office or right from your smart phone or laptop.

Try to inspect as many different house styles that you can. Don't limit yourself to newer homes. Old houses are important to get to know. Older houses present many challenges. Over the years, old houses change with the times and components need to be updated. Coal furnaces get upgraded to fuel oil. Fuel oil furnaces get updated to gas or electric. Old houses might have knob and tube electrical wiring, which is considered hazardous.

Back in the 1970's we found out that lead paint being used in houses was hazardous. Children who played around the paint chips and flakes that fell off painted surfaces were getting lead poisoning from ingesting the chips. Houses built prior to 1978 may contain lead paint. Keep this in mind. If you're having trouble finding the age of the house, a good place to look is under the toilet tank cover. There is always a date of manufacture stamped underneath. Just make sure the toilet wasn't added at a later time.

At one time products that contained asbestos were popular for use in homes. Asbestos can be found in old tile floors, insulation wrap, and siding. At the time it was thought to be a durable product, and it definitely was. We now know that asbestos causes cancer and we no longer use it in homes.

By the time you have done 3 or 4 full practice home inspections you should be gaining confidence and experience. At this point you're probably ready to start taking practice exams. As I told you before, you can find these online. Take the tests over and over until you can pass them with little trouble. There is a home inspection test that is universally accepted by most states and communities for obtaining licensing. This test is called the National Home Inspectors Examination. This test is considered the standard for measuring a home inspectors' knowledge. The test is not free; there is a fee to take it. Go online and research it. If you can pass this exam you will most likely qualify to take any local truth in sale of housing exam or state license exam.

Tools of the Trade

There are a few basic tools that you need to take along on your first inspection. Some of the home inspection schools would have you believe that you need to buy their $500 "tool kits". The truth is you really only need a few basic tools to perform most of the items in a home inspection. I suggest bringing along the following:

Ladder-You should start with at least a 5 foot step ladder. You will want to be able the reach an attic hatch with it. When observing roof coverings you might want an up close look from a ladder. Later on, you should invest in a better ladder. If you don't have one, borrow one from someone.

Receptacle tester with GFCI-This is a must for checking electrical outlets for correct wiring. They also indicate outlets that aren't grounded properly. All you do is plug them into an outlet. Orange and red lights in a row indicate if an outlet is good or bad.

Awl or probe- An awl is an instrument or tool with a sharp, pointy tip. During your inspection you should probe areas of wood for suspected damage. If the wood is soft and falls apart, write it up.

Measuring tape-A retractable 16 foot tape is long enough. A 25 foot tape measure is too bulky to carry around with you. Use one to measure insulation depths in the attic and spaces between railings on stairs.

Rubber soled shoes-You need a good pair of shoes or boots with a rubber sole. Not only do you need rubber for good traction, you need rubber to help protect you from electrical shock when working on service panels.

Tool box or belt-It's easy to lose your tools on an inspection. You'll definitely want a tool belt or a small, lightweight toolbox. Keep your tools nearby so you're not running around looking for them.

Voltage detector-This tool measures the presence of electricity in wires. There are two probes. Stick each one in an outlet to see if it's live.

Binoculars-Use these to get an up close look at the roof covering. They allow you to see the chimney up close without walking on the roof.

Powerful flashlight-You will need a bright and powerful flashlight. I would bring more than one to an inspection and some spare batteries.

Pens (black ink)-You could use blue ink pens too but I prefer black. It's more professional in my opinion.

Clip board- Depending on what report style you decide to use, you will most likely need a good clipboard. Usually you will print your inspection checklists from a report website and fill them in as you do the inspection.

Inspection reports- Bring a couple extra with you in case you need them. You can't do an inspection without one.

Eye protection-When you're working on the electrical service panel you need to put these on. Sparks could get into your eyes. Don't put your eyesight in jeopardy.

Receipt book-Sometimes your client might pay in cash. Have one of these on hand. You can find a receipt book at an office supply store. As you grow you could upgrade to computerized invoices.

As your business grows you should think about adding more tools and services to your business. Some inspectors specialize in moisture intrusion. This requires expensive cameras that can look inside walls and detect moisture. Some inspectors concentrate on the recent "green" housing movement. After you've been an inspector for a while you can decide if any of these things are for you. Even if you decide you don't want to do these, you will have to add to and upgrade your tools. Some items you might consider, after being in business for a while could be:

4' level -Used to determine if surfaces are level. Levels can be used on floors, walls, ceilings, window casings, and door frames. I also carry a smaller 6" level with me on inspections. You can usually tell if floors are level just by walking on them.

Digital camera – use this to take pictures of problem areas so you can identify them easily in your report. Take the pictures during the inspection. Upload the pictures to your report at the home office. Most report websites have digital photo upload capabilities.

Water pressure gage-Use one of these to measure a home's water supply pressure. Simply screw the gage to a threaded faucet or attach to a sink, then turn the water on full. The water pressure is given in PSI or pounds per square inch.

Drop cloth-You never want to damage a floor or track dirt everywhere during your inspection. Find a couple old blankets and keep them in your vehicles. You can lay them down in crawlspaces before going into them. You can also find tarps at home improvement stores.

Coveralls- If you ever find yourself crawling in tight, dirty places, you'll wish you had a pair. Put them on before you go up into an attic or crawl under a house.

Extendable 3 inch mirror- Great for seeing into tight spaces. Especially when working around furnaces. If you're inspecting a gas water heater, you can check for proper exhausting by placing the mirror a few inches from the draft hood. If the mirror fogs up, there is a problem with the exhaust and you need to investigate it further.

Moisture meter-This tool uses a probe to measure the amount of moisture in materials like wood and concrete. When a material is tested the meter will show the percentage of water in the material. Great for finding wood rot, or checking wet spots on drywall ceilings to see if they're active.

Radon test kit-These can be purchased at any home improvement store and are an easy way to increase revenue. The tester is a simply a canister that you exposed to the basement of a house. You have to come back and get it at a later time. Then you have to send the canister to a lab. The lab sends back the results. Inform the client of the results when you get them.

Uniforms-Being a professional home inspector means looking like a professional home inspector. Design a company logo or take your name and have it put on a golf shirt. Good companies that make shirts can be found on the internet.

Foldable type ladder-These ladders are great. You can fold them into a small size and fit them in your cars backseat or trunk. This type of ladder will be more than adequate to perform any inspection task. The best one I have found is the Little Giant. Cheaper knock-offs are available.

Combustible gas detector-This helpful tool is a hand held device that you wave around gas appliances. It measures the amount of carbon monoxide in the air. These are especially useful around furnaces and hot water heater exhaust hoods.

First-aid kit- Keep one in your vehicle. If you get cut or need medical attention you will be glad you have one. Use the aspirin if you get a bad headache. If you get cut, you need to dress your wounds.

Knee pads-There will be times as a home inspector that you will have to crawl around on your knees. Use them when you crawl in the attic or crawlspace. Save your knees and get a pair.

Compass-Just about every inspection report will ask you what direction the house is facing. You could just look on a map and see but it's good to carry a compass.

Rain suit-You will have to do some of your inspections when it's raining outside. Have 2 rain suits in your vehicle. Use one suit for you and one suit for the client. I actually like inspecting in the rain because you can see where water is leaking as it leaks.

Stud sensor-This tool detects the location of studs that are hidden within walls. It's good to know how many inches apart the studs are built. Closer studs will give you a stronger wall. Get one that detects metal studs and pipes as well.

Magnetic vehicle signs-These not only make you appear more professional, they advertise your business as you drive around.

The tools and items I have mentioned here need further explanation than I have written here. Research each item on your own. Make sure you know how to properly use each item before attempting to use it. This list is just a guideline. More tools may be needed to safely conduct an inspection. Use your own discretion.

The Home Office

One of the great things about being a home inspector is that you get to work out of your own living quarters. It doesn't matter if you live in a house or apartment. All you need is a quiet area where you can set up a table or desk and a file cabinet. Your office is just that, your office. Your clients will most likely never come to your home office, so don't worry about appearances. Many new inspectors make the mistake of buying all kinds of fancy office equipment. All you really need when getting started is the following:

Computer with internet access- Today's home inspector must be connected to the World Wide Web. You have to maintain an online presence. I would get a laptop computer if you don't already have one. In the beginning if you don't have a computer you can sign up and use them for free at your local library.

Printer with FAX- Every office needs a printer and a copier. Report checklists need to be printed every time you inspect a house. Having a FAX number helps make business transactions run smoothly.

Phone- Get a good quality landline with voicemail for the office. You should also carry a cell phone. Today's smart phones have many different applications for home inspectors. They even have home inspection report applications that you fill in on your phone. Tablet style computers are also something to think about. Home inspectors must learn to evolve with the times.

Order forms-These are the sheets you keep by the phone to fill in when someone calls for an inspection. I talked about these earlier.

Business cards-Always carry your business cards on you. These are your calling cards. Give them out at inspections and give to realtors at their office when you visit.

Inspection contracts- Find these online. If you want to make your own you can find examples on the internet. Never do an inspection without a contract.

Postage and shipping supplies-You need postage and envelopes to send out reports to your clients. Get larger "flat" size envelopes as well as regular letter sized envelopes. Think about getting a postage meter when you start doing lots of business.

Desk or table-You have to have a comfortable work space. You don't need anything fancy, just a nice big space to lay out your materials. Make sure you have a good light source

Filing cabinet-You should keep a copy of all the inspections you do for at least two years. Keep everything neat and easy to find. Invest in a quality filing cabinet. If you want one that will last your entire career, buy yourself a Hon brand file cabinet.

Rules and Regulation by State

The amount of red tape and requirements involved in becoming a home inspector depends entirely upon which state where you plan on working. In one state you may need to pass a test and reach certain requirements. In another state you may simply just register your business with the state and hang a sign on your door saying "open for business". The easiest way to learn your states requirements is to log onto a computer and go to your states official website. Go to www.state.xx.us . Instead of typing xx after state, fill in the postal abbreviation for your state. For example, Ohio would be www.state.oh.us. Then follow the website along to the page dealing with home inspector regulations. Check your state carefully because the laws are constantly changing. I lived near the border of two states and had two different sets of rules to follow. Minnesota didn't require being licensed. Wisconsin required every home inspector to be licensed. I went to Wisconsin and took a state administered test. After I passed it, my license was sent to me in the mail. At this point I was legally able to perform home inspections in Wisconsin

Insurance you will need to carry

Before you go out and actually do real home inspections for pay make sure you have insurance. It might be tempting to save money and not carry insurance. Don't do business this way. You never know when a gust of wind might blow your ladder off the side of the roof, and onto someone else's car. If you fell through a ceiling without insurance, you would be paying out of your own pocket. In many areas it's illegal to operate without insurance. If you are trying to get a truth in housing inspector license, they will ask for proof of insurance. This part of your insurance coverage is called business liability insurance.

The other type of insurance you need is called errors and omissions insurance. E and O insurance covers you for items you might miss during an inspection. It also would cover anything you might misidentify. If you write in a report that a roof is real slate and it turns out to be manufactured slate, you will be responsible for replacing that roof with real slate. The price difference in real slate is several thousand more dollars. You can get a monthly policy or a "per inspection" policy. Check around on the internet. There are plenty of insurance companies on there.

Obviously you wouldn't want to drive to an inspection without having coverage on your vehicle. Make your current auto insurance covers any inspection work you do. Talk to your agent and find out.

Free and Low Cost Ways to Get Started

During my process of becoming a home inspector I discovered many free or low cost ideas to help get your business going. Business cards are an essential part of your business. There are a lot of printing companies out there that can print you business cards. Because of all the competition out there, many companies are offering free business cards to draw you in as a customer. Do an online search and find a good printing company. Design your own cards on their webpage and have them printed up and sent. I got my first 1000 cards for free.

As I mentioned earlier, you can get free or low cost inspection reports on the internet. The same websites that offer electronic reports usually let you have space on their site to create your own webpage. This at least gives you internet exposure and a virtual address. I suggest you take a look at the website Reporthost.com or the website Homegage.com.

There are quite a few ways to get exposure on the internet. When people do a search for home inspectors in your area, you want your name to come up on their search. An easy way to find out where you can list is to do an internet search for home inspectors in your area. Look at the websites that pop up on the search. Go to each one and go to the sites homepage. They usually have a section to click on called "add me to your directory". Sometimes getting on these lists is free. Other times you will need to pay a fee.

Websites like Craigslist are places you can offer your services. Don't expect tons of business from any one of these suggestions alone. Try every possible way you can think of. The longer you have been around and the more exposure you get, the more people will know about you and use you for inspections

Using Realtors to Your Advantage

Realtors can be a great source for home inspection work. Get to know some of the realtors in your area. The way I did this was by driving around the area and stopping in at every realty office I could find. I would walk up to the receptionist and tell her who I was and that I just wanted to leave some information about myself and my inspections. I had a printed up flyer that I put in every realtors mailbox along with my business card and a new customer discount offer. If you ask politely the receptionist will usually let you walk around and meet realtors around the office.

Another place to meet realtors one on one is at an open house. Look up open houses in the newspaper or online. Go to each one and go inside and introduce yourself to the realtor. If they are busy wait for a slow moment to talk to them. In any case I would leave a few business cards on the kitchen table. A prospective buyer might see your card and grab one.

Affiliations

Being part of affiliations can give your business an advantage over others. Customers like to know that you are part of a select group of individuals. It definitely adds credibility to your business. In order to join an affiliation you must pay a yearly fee and adhere to their strict home inspecting guidelines. You start out as a candidate and work up to full member status. In order to reach full member status, you must do a set number of inspections as a candidate. Sometimes this could be as many as 200 inspections or more. Two of the best affiliations to join are the American Society of Home Inspectors (ASHI) and the National Association of Home Inspectors (NAHI). Go look on their websites for more information.

Standards and Integrity

As a home inspector you must operate with a high set of moral standards. Before you go out and charge actual clients for inspections, make sure you are completely and properly trained. It wouldn't be fair for you do a sloppy or incomplete inspection for a paying client. If you're not ready, go back and study some more. Remember that home inspectors are considered generalist and are not expected to be experts in everything. Home inspectors should know a little bit about a lot of things. This is the reason that we call in the experts when we uncover issues. If the service panel looks wrong, write it up and add that an electrician needs to be called out for a further look. If the foundation looks bad, write it up, tell them to call in a structural engineer. You call out the problems; they come out, investigate, diagnose and repair.

When you do each inspection you should be doing it as if you were buying the house yourself. Never let anyone talk you into covering up a problem. Always report exactly what you see. If you cover up problems you are being dishonest and may end up paying for it when it's discovered.

Being a home inspector can be a challenging and rewarding career. Always stay on top of things by keeping up with the latest construction techniques. Being a licensed inspector does require you to take continuing education on a yearly basis. Sign up for home inspector seminars and get your credits. To stay informed, I like watching the DIY network on cable TV. This Old House is a great series for learning construction techniques. Keep yourself informed and remember, you could be making $100 dollars an hour doing home inspections.

Disclaimer

Inspecting houses and owning your own business requires more research and knowledge than you can obtain from my book alone. You should hire your own attorney and have them look over your company and business plan before you open for business. The author and publisher do not assume and hereby disclaim any liability to any party for any loss or damage caused by errors and omissions in You Could Be Making $100 an Hour Doing Home Inspections, whether such errors or omissions result from accident or any other cause.

www.ingramcontent.com/pod-product-compliance
Lightning Source LLC
Chambersburg PA
CBHW071610170526
45166CB00003B/1043